DEALING WITH WOMEN

BOOK 2

THE LACK OF REASON

By.

Richard Longshanks

DEALING WITH WOMEN THE LACK OF REASON

First edition. February 21, 2018.

Written by Richard Longshanks.

For all of the men who have been falsely accused and or convicted without a trial.

PROLOGUE

1

These words were written over a century ago by a man whose teachings have all but been banned. He told the crystal truth about women in such a way that it frightened men, the idea that women could be so consciously evil. His writings chilled women to their cold little hearts because they knew that a man had finally brushed aside their painted veil and told the world what lurched behind all of the soft words and makeup. His name was Arthur Schopenhauer. You should study his teaching as great generals of the past studied the Art Of War. This is a quote from one of his essays.

- Hence, it will be found that the fundamental fault of the female character is that it has *no sense of justice*. This is mainly due to the fact, already mentioned, that women are defective in the powers of reasoning and deliberation; but it is also traceable to the position which Nature has assigned to them as the weaker sex. They are dependent, not upon strength, but upon craft; and hence their instinctive capacity for cunning, and their ineradicable tendency to say what is not true. For as lions are provided with claws and teeth, and elephants and boars with tusks, bulls with horns, and cuttle fish with its clouds of inky fluid, so Nature has equipped woman, for her defence and protection, with the arts of dissimulation; and all the power which Nature has conferred upon man in the shape of physical strength and reason, has been bestowed upon women in this form. Hence, dissimulation is innate in woman, and almost as much a quality of the stupid as of the clever. - Arthur Schopenhauer

CHAPTER ONE THEY WERE WARNED

- NEVER LET THE FUTURE disturb you. You will meet it, if you have to, with the same weapons of reason which today arm you against the present.

-Marcus Aurelius

Remember that moment in As Good As it Gets when Jack explains how he is able to write about women so convincingly and he says that he starts with a man and then takes away all accountability and reason.

For those of us who have gone through the wars, we knew how true that statement was. For the rest, of men on this planet, they needed a wake-up call. They needed to see how totally irrational these creature could get.

Jump to the year 2017.

In an effort that can only be described as self-emulation women decided on mass to accuse any and every single man in sight of sexual harassment and or abuse.

Are some of these guys guilty?

Sure.

Are all of them?

No way.

But in this new world being created by women if you are accused of something you are guilty as charged and we need to skip the trial and defense so that we can jump to the sentencing phase. In this alien world, this Me/Too world, this world that bears no resemblance to reality all of mankind are looking to take advantage of these sweet and delicate flowers that we call women.

The end result from this all out assault on men is that in the short term many an innocent man are going to suffer greatly. However, over the long term, women are the ones who have done permanent damage to their position in society.

Trust a woman?

Out the window.

Give a woman the benefit of the doubt?

Out the window.

Allow yourself to be alone with a woman that you work with?

Fuck no.

Dating a female co-worker?

Only the low IQ guys would even consider that from this point on.

Allow me, your humble scribe to look at this in purely Vulcan logic terms over the next few chapter.

CHAPTER TWO THESE BOOKS

- LAW IS NOTHING OTHER than a certain ordinance of reason for the common good, promulgated by the person who has the care of the community.

-Thomas Aquinas

Before I continue I have to tell you that my last book, Dealing with Women and Their BS, The Bluff, was well received by you guys. While women hated it. They gave it bad reviews and even managed to slow down the publishing of it at every turn. So if you want to read or listen to more of these books at Audible please leave reviews and share this book with every man you meet.

The feedback that I received from women about my previous book came down to either shaming tactics or emotional babel. Nonsense like, you will never have a committed relationship with a real woman. What the hell is a real woman? Do they even know?

Are we talking about women that existed before the age of feminism?

To find those women I would need a time machine.

Are we talking about women who have not been infected by the virus of the self centered self absorbed materialistic females that populate the west?

To all of the ladies in the audience, this comes from the bottom of my heart, the answer is no. I am not here to please you. I am not here to tell other men how to win your cold little hearts. I am not going to encourage men to act more like women so that they can be used and abused by the weaker and lesser sex.

Today I kick over the card table and these game that we have been playing is being reset for a reality check.

CHAPTER THREE MEN AREN'T STUPID

I love the man that can smile in trouble, that can gather strength from distress, and grow brave by reflection. 'Tis the business of little minds to shrink, but he whose heart is firm, and whose conscience approves his conduct, will pursue his principles unto death. -Thomas Paine

IF A MAN STICKS HIS hand in a fire he learns quickly that fire will burn him and he will not do that again.

If he sees a man sticking his hand in a fire and getting burnt he will learn from the injury that the man suffers and that he should avoid doing that.

This is the basic law of cause and effect. It is a law governed by logic.

Women are emotional creatures. They do not care for logic. They believe that logic is mean. Logic is hateful. Women allow their emotions to run wild with not care about the laws of cause and effect.

On an emotional level it is okay to accuse every man of every manner of evil whether they did it or not so that said men will learn through the emotional experience that women need to be valued more.

What a load of self destructive bullshit.

When have men ever in the history of this world responded by retreating to our emotions and becoming more like women.

When men are attacked unfairly we retreat. Then we regroup. We figure out the motives and the tactics of our enemy and then we responded with overwhelming firepower.

We are going to look at the tactic that they have used over the last few month. We are going to responded with cold clear logic and this will change the world that they have lived cradled and safely in forever. This logical response is going to drive them crazy.

Now let us look at the way we are being attacked.

The Tactic: The Accusation. This is a powerful tactic that has taken out men at all levels. From the guy on the street to men working in the White House.

Men are being accused usually in the workplace.

To all the men who decided during this pass holiday season to cancel all work and office parties, way to go guys.

Parties to women are like Bowl games to men and ending this social interaction is a good start. A chance at getting laid is not worth a lawsuit or a lost career. Being alone with women after hours is out of the questions from now until the end of time. That bridge is burnt and will never be rebuilt.

"But guys we look forward to these parties every year. Dancing and getting to know that eligible VP after hours is something we look forward to", a woman would say.

While I would counter, "that is too damn bad baby. You did this to yourself. If you want to dance and have a party then all of you ladies can do it by yourselves. Be a feminist, women do not need men and men need women who are co-workers like a coffin needs a nail. Fuck off and go have a scissor pity party with the ugly chicks who invented this crap back in the 1960s."

Now allow me to whisper something that many women think, but few will ever say aloud.

Women are not as good at work as men.

Most women believe that work begins at nine and ends at five. Most men believe that work ends when the job gets done.

Men take pride in getting shit done while women take pride in having shown up. They take pride in the appearance of things rather than the lasting reality. Because of this women are going to find it harder and harder to find work alongside men. If I ran a large corporation and it came down between a choice of being fined by the government for not hiring women or hiring women I would eat the fines. You can logically factor in the risk of fines. While having a bunch of female cancer cells drifting around the office could sink the entire company. Men are realizing that sometimes you must cut off the pink pinkie finger to say the strong hand.

But WOMEN are more EDUCATED than their male counterparts. This is valuable to a company right?

Not really.

It is like basic algebra. Education equals X and it depends on how you define X. Well men and women define X differently.

Well Richard, who is correct in their definition?

Men of course.

Women miss the point of what an education is actually for.

This is why women look at education as a goal and once they have a piece of paper that says that they put in four years and got their BS degree they have conquered the world. Men on the other hand look at learning a skill or trade as the end goal. We understand that a piece of paper is something you use to wipe your ass with when you are broken and no one wants a liberal arts major. Liberal arts is not even a real thing. If I ran a college I would give out four year degrees in Magic. Why not? Magic is about as useful in the real world as liberal arts. Women fail to understand that a skill or a trade will put food on the table and pay the bills every single day. To put it in simple terms a women seeks validation from others while a man finds validation only in the end result.

This is why women who are attacking men in the workplace are insanely happy to bath in the glory and spotlight that other women shine on them for a few moments while not think about the end result of their insane Me Too movement.

Oh look, every man is a predator.

Oh look, every single man is out to exploit me.

This is going to soon turn into.

Oh no, there is not a man who will hire me.

Oh no, no man is willing to interact with me.

Oh no, I am a tired old wall crashed no talent like Rose McGowan pathetically trying to be relevant in a world that passed me by back when a guy named Bush was president.

Oh my, I should go out and adopt an elderly cat so that there are two old pussies in my one room apartment that no one wants anything to do with instead of one.

Authors note: Men, at this point you should write and post your review of this book to counter the nuclear hate I am going to get from the girls. They killed the last gospel that I wrote because too many one star reviews get a book taken down on most Ebook platforms.

CHAPTER FOUR THE PAMPERED

Since the days of noble knights in shining armor the most over pampered, overprotected, over indulged and overrated creature in the history of the world has been the little white girl.

You know the hero of countless fictional stories. Saving the universe with their lightsabers without ever even having read the instruction manual that came with the laser sword. This boney bitches cannot program a remote or change a tire, but dammit when push comes to shove they can kick Darth Vader's ass and single handedly win the Infinity War. The little white girl who is both commando and all purpose victim. The Swiss army knife of contradictions.

When you need someone to save your ass, don't call a navy seal, call a little white girl.

When you need a superhero, don't call superman, call a little white girl who can flip over tanks one minute and in the next minute file a massive lawsuit against the director for staring at her lack of tits for a moment too long.

(God in heaven, Lynda Carter was so much hotter it makes me want to scream)

Okay, I am back.

(No, I am gone again. I am not done with the Wonder Woman film. How can they have an island of Amazon women and only two or three are worth a second look. And what the hell happened to the Princess Bride? How did she end up looking like an old man? What happened to her pretty face after hitting the wall is totally inconceivable.)

These physical and mental giants carved civilization out of the wilderness didn't they?

Dammit, that was man wasn't it?

They pushed back darkness by learning the secret of fire right?

No?

Who did that?

A man.

That makes more sense.

Electricity?

The wheel?

The boat?

The car?

The airplane?

Was it a woman in drag?

Was it one of the powerpuff girls?

Here is a hint at the answer.

It was those creatures that first walked on the moon and thanks to all the craps that women pile on them, die too soon.

It was men.

Grown ass men.

Music.

Art.

Law.

Science.

Facebook.

The iPhone.

The internet.

And coming soon androids to replace the females of a species that is dominated by the achievements of the males.

Damn, it feels good to be a gangster.

CHAPTER FIVE PROTECTING YOURSELVES

"LIFE IS A STORM, MY young friend. You will bask in the sunlight one moment, be shattered on the rocks the next. What makes you a man is what you do when that storm comes. You must look into that storm and shout as you did in Rome. Do your worst, for I will do mine! Then the fates will know you as we know you" - Alexandre Dumas

Men must learn to protect themselves at all cost. If you allow yourself to drop your guard around the enemy then you could lose your career and maybe even your freedom.

The enemy?

You do not really mean that women are our enemies?

Anyone who constantly speak in terms of fighting is not a friend. Do not allow yourselves to be fooled by their painted faces.

They trade in lies. They live to perfect their ability to deceive. When they speak of justice it is always framed in terms of envy.

They say that women should make as much as men, but not one of them have ever suggested that women go out and do the dangerous jobs that men do.

From rigging power lines to working on oil rigs men dominate these high paying jobs. These jobs are open to any and all, but little white girls are not lining up to work on top of oil rigs in the middle of the Atlantic when it is forty degrees below zero and a storm is rolling in.

I am not saying that women cannot do these jobs. I am saying (quoting a hero of mine) "What we have here is a lack of guts."

They can talk shit, but do not want to do the hard shit?

On the off chance they were willing to do this kind of work I am sure that these industries would be overwhelmed by a flood of lawsuits after all men who do that kind of work must be the most macho and sexism jerks on planet earth. In the world of the accuser; Men who have dirty hands, must automatically have dirty minds.

If you wake up one day guys and find that your male workspace has been invaded by a women it is time to establish you defenses as soon as possible and on as many fronts a possible.

I have been joking around up until this point, but it is time to get serious.

In this new Me/Too universe your careers, your lives and your reputations are on the chopping block. You could lose it all and your freedom too.

Men are sitting in jail for crimes that they did not even think about committing. Innocent men rotting away because they got on the wrong side of a women.

Here is what you are going to have to be prepared to do to protect yourself.

Like dealing with any other kind of virus the best option is to avoid it at all cost. If you can avoid being near them or at all cost alone with a women in the workplace you need to do just that. Alone mean automatically if any accusations are made then it becomes a he said she said and she will always win because the legal system and public opinion favors the female.

Whenever possible you should invite a third party to be present or a group of fellow workers. You can plan ahead for this opinion with other male co-workers. A simple signal to another man or men at work can been arranged so that if or when the moment comes that you may have to go into an office or even an elevator alone with a women at work they will automatically join you.

You know what it is like? There is this old episode of Star Trek where this hot female android is sent to kill a crew member. She is programmed to be able to only kill him so she would say something like I am here for Mike and when when she touched Mike he would die, but if she touched anyone else nothing happened. So when she came for McCoy Kirk could step in and protect the doc from the android. Then when she came for Kirk Sulu could step in and save Kirk. The key to this is that there needs to be at least two men present to protect the target from the evil android chick at all times.

If this is unavailable to you then you need to record every single meeting. You can download some great dictation recording apps to your phone. You can get great audio and some will also give you a written transcript. Visual evidence is even better, but you will probably need to talk that over with management before you can install surveillance.

Okay, what if you have an argument or disagreement with a woman at work?

You need to immediately report it to human services. You want to be the one who reports it and have your name on it first. This gives you control of the narrative later. The odds are that the woman was the one who started the drama because that is what they are, drama queens.

"Hey, you want me to play the victim Richard?"

No. In this case you are the victim or if you do not heed my warning, you will be the victim. You need to cover your asses gentlemen. If you do not you may find yourself being treated rougher than fresh fish at the state prison. Women will not hesitate to screw you raw and without lube if you get caught bending over in front of them. Do not give them the chance. Do not get fucked because you are trying to be a nice guy or avoiding being a snitch.

They are from Venus.

They are not human like us!

They do not respect the concept of rules or honor. When it comes to victimizing innocent men they cannot wait to chime in me too.

CHAPTER SIX MARCHING ORDERS

25

—

- Wars may be fought with weapons, but they are won by men. It is the spirit of men who follow and of the man who leads that gains the victory. - George S. Patton

Richard will we survive this war that they have started with man? Guys it will not be easy.

It will not happen in days or weeks. It will take years and our generation may rise and fall before we win this conflict. Our enemy will sink to any level. They will crawl lower than the lowest slime.

They will lie and backstab and play every dirt game and pull every rotten trick known and perhaps invent some new ones. They will get desperate when they realize that their reign of tyranny is nearing an end.

For generations uncounted we sought to make women our equals. We put them above us in so many ways. We offered them our love, our protection from this cold unfeeling world. We made them the centers of our universe. We trusted them. We believed in them. We gave them control over our finances. We gave them sway over raising the children. We took this ball of blue spinning spinning spinning through eternity and turned it into the cradle of known civilization.

We are not children to be lectured to.

We are not predators to be put into a made up category.

We do not have to become more like women to become better men.

We are already the best thing in the long history of creation. At our best we shine as bright as the angels and only fall short of our all powerful creator.

We have been kicked.

We have been blamed.

We have been marginalized.

We have been put through it and gone through it. The roughest is yet to come and the pain has only begun. We as men will endure this. We will survive it and we will win in the end. This is just another moment when we are tested. This time it is bitch testing and shit testing. This is no different from the ice age, the dark age, the stone age and that really bizarre age when men wore wigs. (What the hell was that about?)

They call all the times that have passed and all of the time yet to come history.

Women over look that simple fact. That the story of existence on planet earth was, is and forever shall be: His Story.

May god bless you merry gentlemen.

Your humble scribe,

Richard Longshanks

Don't miss out!

Click the button below and you can sign up to receive emails whenever Richard Longshanks publishes a new book. There's no charge and no obligation.

https://books2read.com/r/B-A-MZVE-GFPR

BOOKS 2 READ

Connecting independent readers to independent writers.

Did you love *Dealing With Women The Lack of Reason*? Then you should read *Call Her Bluffs* by Richard Longshanks!

Dealing with Women is something that we Men have been trying to do since the beginning of time. **They play games** and these games have no rules except winning at any cost. We cannot expect them to play fair, but what we can do is **learn how to recognize their Bluffs** and show that they are always holding the losing hand.

Whether you have been with her for five days or five years the signs will be the same because their playbook is universal. **Women will test you.** Women will play games with you. Women will push your buttons and do what ever it takes to take control of the relationship.

With this books I hope to teach you guys about one of their most time worn tools. **The bluff.** When all else fails they will reach for the chips and threaten to leave or to cry or to cut you off.

How often have you fallen for one of those bluffs and given her want she wants. They will bluff you and make you give up something that you love or love to do. The thing that has been hidden behind their theatrics is the fact that **you always hold the winning hand**. If you do not fold you will always win.

Guys let's face it constantly losing these pointless battles stinks.

Just because they have been winning does not mean that it has to continue.

Every Bluff has a tell and I am going to show you how to recognize them.

This is no ordinary relationship book. Anyone can write one of those feel good let's hold hands and everything is going to be all right candy ass books. You know what, most of those books have been written by women hiding behind male pen names. You can always tell because they constantly preach that you much change yourself and become a sensitive flower that can relate to her feelings.

Also by Richard Longshanks

a man's guide
Dealing With Women The Lack of Reason
Call Her Bluffs